Princess Briana

Author
Yaba Baker

Illustrator
Javier C. Gonzalez III

Second Edition – Second Printing
June 2007

ISBN: 978-1-928889-06-9

Dedicated to my Grandma (Daisy Bell Williams)
August 16, 1905 – June 27, 2004

My grandmother was a living example of God's principles. She began serving God in 1929. She fed the hungry (out of her own kitchen many times), took care of the sick and the elderly until she was almost 80 years old. Grandma worked tirelessly in her church seven days a week. She raised her own seven children, as well as a host of nieces, nephews, grandchildren, great grandchildren, great-great grandchildren and even children in the neighborhood.

My grandma was my daily example of how to live my life for Christ; not in word but in deed. She strongly believed that love is the key. Until her death at the age of 98, her actions exemplified love. She possessed the loving qualities that we should all strive to attain. My grandma's favorite quote was "All I see, I love, and none I hate." We should all adopt her favorite quote in our daily lives.

Many years ago, in a country called Eseryia, there lived a princess named Briana. Throughout the world, Eseryia was known to be the wealthiest and most beautiful country in the history of man. The land overflowed with all types of trees, lovely flowers and rich fruits and vegetables. Precious stones and metals, like diamonds, rubies, emeralds, gold, and silver, were plentiful in Eseryia.

Criden, the king of Eseryia, ruled the kingdom alongside his beautiful queen, Ayon. The king and queen were not satisfied until every citizen had a home with food on the table. They ruled the kingdom with love and declared, "Every man, woman, and child of Eseryia shall have a full stomach and a roof over their head every night."

The king and queen had wealth, fame, and every type of luxury, but the one part of their life they were the most proud of was their daughter, Briana. She was the most beautiful, intelligent princess in the world.

One day a messenger came to the castle to deliver a letter for Princess Briana. The message came with an invitation from a school called Elite, which was located in Spain.

The message read: "Dear Princess Briana, News of your beauty and intelligence has traveled throughout the world. Therefore, you have been invited to attend Elite's exclusive summer camp for princesses, located in Spain."

The royal couple thought it would be an excellent chance for Briana to learn about other cultures. She was twelve years old and had been on many journeys to other countries, but she had never been out of Africa. The best scholars in the world taught Briana math, science, and philosophy. She also learned how to play instruments from world-famous musical geniuses.

Briana was excited about traveling to another continent for the first time. She smiled as she thought about meeting new people and learning new languages.

"I can't believe I'm going to Europe!" she shouted.

As Briana prepared for her trip, she thought about being away from her parents for three months, and how much she would miss them, but a few days later she hugged and kissed her parents and joined the royal procession aboard the ship to sail to Elite.

After a long journey by sea and a short one on land, Princess Briana's royal procession arrived at Elite. In front of the school stood a guide appointed to greet the princess. When Princess Briana entered the main hall, she noticed many paintings of young ladies about her age hung on the walls.

"Each young lady on the wall was the top princess for the summer she attended camp," explained the guide. "Every summer there is a yearly competition among different camps. Every year, for the past 100 years, Elite has won top honors."

The guide continued, "The school has had a portrait of each winner painted to hang in this grand hall. Queen Hatcher holds the top score in the history of the competition. She teaches here at Elite." As Briana looked at the paintings, she saw that none of them looked like her. Briana's eyes and skin were brown, and her hair was kinky and braided. Every princess had white skin, long straight hair and blue or green eyes.

Princess Briana quietly wondered, "Do I belong here?"

Briana looked out onto a courtyard filled with people and was shocked that there were no other African princesses in the entire school. She was sure that some of her friends from other African kingdoms would have been invited. Yet, to her surprise, they had not. She began to feel like an outsider.

"I should never have come to this place," sighed Briana.

As many weeks passed, Briana got settled in and even made some new friends. With just six weeks left in the program she was very homesick and looked forward to seeing her parents. Briana had done very well in her other classes and was looking forward to her next and final class, Queen Hatcher's Beauty Instruction for the Elite Princess. Queen Hatcher's score of 97 points was the highest ever in the summer competition, and Briana was anxious to learn all she could from her.

Briana's eyes sparkled with enthusiasm as she entered the classroom. All the princesses were whispering excitedly. Briana leaned over to the princess of Italy.

"I've been looking forward to this class," she whispered.

"Me too," Princess Antonia squealed excitedly.

The room became quiet as Queen Hatcher glided in.

"She's so classy and elegant," Briana thought to herself. Queen Hatcher began the lesson by setting up a poster about beauty.

"A proper princess," began Queen Hatcher, "should have hair that is long and straight, and skin that is a perfect peach color. The best color for the eyes is blue."

A princess sitting behind Briana raised her hand to ask about brown eyes.

"If you have brown eyes," replied Queen Hatcher, "you will just have to make do with what you have, won't you? She continued, "a princess should be no larger than a perfect size two at all times."

As the class ended, Princess Antonia stood beside the poster that Queen Hatcher had placed in front of the class. She said, "Most of us look nothing like this poster. I don't have blue eyes or blonde hair, and I am not a size two. Queen Hatcher and her poster are saying that I'm ugly."

Briana spoke up. "I don't think Queen Hatcher is saying that this is the only type of beauty, just one of many ways a young princess can be beautiful." Princess Antonia did not agree with Briana. The two princesses decided that Briana would go to Queen Hatcher and ask her.

She went to Queen Hatcher's office after class to talk about the lesson.

Princess Briana asked, "Did you really mean that a proper princess could look only like your poster?"

Queen Hatcher spoke in a very harsh tone, "Briana, if you are not the right size, and do not have the hair, eyes, or skin color to be an Elite princess that is not my fault. Perhaps you are just not Elite material." Briana felt terrible after listening to Queen Hatcher.

She was so hurt by Queen Hatcher's words that she ran from the room. She didn't know what to do or who to turn to. She had never felt like this in her life. "Is there something wrong with the way I look? The answer has to be yes. Queen Hatcher knows beauty. She is the top teacher in the school. How can she be wrong?" Briana thought. "I don't want to be African anymore," sobbed Briana. "I don't want my hair, my eyes, or my skin color. I want to change it all!"

Briana knew that she had to do something. She decided that she would do anything to look like that poster. She would do anything not to feel so alone, ugly, and most of all, like an outsider. "I've got to do something. Anything is better than feeling so ugly."

Briana decided that if she was going to be a size two, she had to stop eating. She skipped dinner and snuck into the chemistry lab.

"I should be able to find everything I need in here," said Briana. She chose the chemicals she thought would straighten her hair and make it lighter. After thinking for a moment, she decided she would also need more chemicals to mix a powder that would make her skin lighter too.

Hours later, Briana looked into a mirror to discover that she had made a mess. She hadn't brought her chemistry notes from home and didn't know which chemicals to mix. Instead of the dark brown, soft, tight coils she used to have, her hair was nearly green, rough and spiked. The powder Briana had mixed for her skin looked like a mask that didn't match her skin well.

"Well," Briana thought, "this is better than the old Briana." She headed to the courtyard where the other princesses went to practice their poise, go over lessons, or relax after class. Briana decided this would be the perfect time to show everyone that she was beginning to fit in and show off her new look. She smiled as she entered the courtyard. Briana expected surprised smiles from the other princesses, but as they began to notice her, she thought she heard a giggle. In minutes, the courtyard was filled with roaring laughter.

Confused and embarrassed, Briana ran from the courtyard, crying so hard she could not see. As Briana sped through the grand hall, she bumped into someone. Briana wiped her eyes and looked up to see a beautiful African queen looking down at her. Looking at the queen, Briana was sure she would have remembered if she had met her before.

Briana whispered, "Who are you?"

"I am Queen Zorra," she answered. "And who are you?"

Feeling shy, Briana quietly answered, "My name is Princess Briana."

Queen Zorra asked, "Why are you crying, Princess Briana?" Briana was embarrassed, but she had to be respectful and answer the queen.

"Everybody was laughing at me because I'm African," sighed Briana.

The queen looked puzzled by Briana's answer.

"Do you really think they were laughing at you because you are African?"

"Yes!" Briana answered.

"The children were not laughing at you because you are African. They were laughing because you are trying to be something you are not," the queen gently explained to Briana.

"Queen Zorra," Briana responded, "I want to be a beautiful princess, an Elite princess."

Queen Zorra smiled and said, "But you are a beautiful princess."

"Queen Hatcher doesn't think so!" snapped Briana. "I don't look anything like her chart of beauty."

"Oh, now I see," said Queen Zorra, "because you don't look like a poster or a picture that someone else thinks is beautiful, then you are not beautiful? Come with me child." Queen Zorra motioned for her assistants to follow her and Princess Briana into the guest quarters. The assistants began to work on Briana's skin and hair while Queen Zorra continued speaking. "Briana, you must learn to love yourself, and this means loving every part of you. You are one of God's beautiful creations. He doesn't make mistakes. You have beautiful hair, eyes, and skin."

"But Queen Hatcher's chart says I'm ugly," interrupted Briana.

"Who is Queen Hatcher to judge beauty? True beauty exists only when a person loves who he or she is without seeking the approval of others. If you love yourself, people can feel your energy. They begin to sense your happiness, your belief in yourself, and your inner beauty.

Once that happens, your other features like hair, eyes, and skin begin to catch the attention of everybody. Never let anyone else tell you whether you are beautiful or not. If God created you, then you are beautiful. Never forget that!"

Briana felt so much better after spending time with Queen Zorra. She felt like her old self again, confident, beautiful, and intelligent, like nothing could stop her. Briana was no longer trying to change herself to fit Queen Hatcher's idea of beauty. She was proud of her dark brown skin, kinky braided hair, and lovely brown eyes. She loved who she was on the inside as well as what she looked like on the outside. Princess Briana decided right then that she would never try to change herself to fit in or judge herself by other people's ideas.

It was time for the annual competition. Princes and princesses from different camps in Europe came to compete to be the top prince and princess. Briana was excited about entering. When she went to apply, all the teachers laughed at her request, Queen Hatcher laughed the loudest.

"Ha-Ha-Ha! You must be joking. You need a queen to be your sponsor if you want to compete. Believe me, no one is going to sponsor someone who looks like you."

"Oh really," said a voice from the other side of the room. "I wouldn't be so sure about that, Queen Hatcher." Briana turned to see Queen Zorra, who said, "I would be pleased to sponsor Princess Briana in the competition."

Queen Hatcher would not dare challenge Queen Zorra. She frowned but gave Briana an application.

THE TOP PRINCE AND PRINCESS

It was the day of the competition, and Princess Briana was a little nervous. The competition was made up of five parts. Each contestant had to take tests in math, science, philosophy, and showcase a talent. The only part she was worried about was the section on beauty. Briana loved the way she looked, but what if the judges agreed with Queen Hatcher's poster?

When Princess Briana heard the applause, she knew the competition had begun. She was surprised to hear a familiar voice, and looked up to see Queen Zorra on the stage. She was the mistress of ceremonies. Briana grinned as she hurried to take her seat for the tests. Briana had learned science, math, and philosophy from the greatest minds in the world, her African teachers. She was confident as she answered each question.

The judges were amazed to see a young lady breeze through tests that give the best scientists and philosophers a hard time. In the talent competition, the judges were dazzled by Princess Briana's musical ability. She played the piano with the skill of an adult concert pianist.

It was the end of the day, and every Prince and Princess had finished all parts of the competition. The time came for the judges' decision on who would be the champion prince and princess. An envelope was handed from the judges to Queen Zorra. As Queen Zorra stood and opened the envelope, Princess Briana felt butterflies in her stomach.

"This moment seems to be taking forever," thought Briana.
"And the winner is," announced Queen Zorra, "Princess Briana!"
"I won?" Briana was shocked. "I won!" she shouted.

Queen Zorra explained how the judges came to their decision. "Princess Briana not only showed magnificent talent on the piano by playing a difficult piece beautifully, but she made history by becoming the first princess to ever get a perfect score of 100 on all her tests."

One of the judges stood and spoke excitedly.

"Princess Briana's talent and intelligence were more than enough to win the competition. What really made it no contest was her stunning beauty. As judges, we look for contestants that believe in themselves, have positive energy, and have confidence.

"Too often, young princesses value the way they look more than any of their other qualities." The judge explained, "We could see in Princess Briana's smile that there is something special about her. We could feel her positive energy and see that, with her beautiful hair, sparkling eyes, and wonderful skin color, she is clearly the most intelligent, skillful, and beautiful young woman in this competition. Princess Briana by far is the top princess in the world."

The time had come for all of the Elite students to return to their kingdoms. As Princess Briana prepared to leave, she looked around her room to be sure that nothing was left behind. After leaving the building, she spotted Queen Hatcher's royal carriage riding away with all her belongings. As she was saying goodbye to her guide, Briana asked why Queen Hatcher was leaving.

"Teachers at Elite," the guide explained, "are supposed to help our students see the beauty in themselves. Once the principal found out what Queen Hatcher did to you and other students, she was promptly asked to leave."

As Princess Briana walked down the grand hall one last time, she stopped to look at her painting. Princess Briana had replaced Queen Hatcher as the top princess in history. She silently wished Queen Hatcher well. Her father, King Criden, always said that hate did the most damage to the one who held on to it. "And besides," thought Briana, "if I'm going to stay positive and love myself, I can't be bothered with hating others." Princess Briana hurried outside, anxious to get home and share all that she had learned.

Briana
Top Princess In History

www.princessbriana.com

Visit me online! Learn more about my kingdom and how you too can become a princess or prince by joining the **Princess Briana Royalty Club**. Just go to www.princessbriana.com and begin your journey to becoming an official princess or prince. Join now and you will receive a personal email from me every month!

Join the Princess Briana Royalty Club Today and Receive:

 Monthly emails from Princess Briana

 A chance to win prizes

 Your picture featured on the website (some restrictions apply)

Connect with other members of the Princess Briana Royalty Club

 Princess Creed

I, _____ (say your name), from this day forward I will love myself and believe in myself. I am beautiful, smart, and talented. I will never let anyone tell me different. I am humble, respectful of other people, and treat other people as I want to be treated. I have the ability to do great things in life. All these qualities will guide my life as a princess. From this day forward I will be known as Princess _____ (say your name).

The words above are the official princess creed. Recite these words every morning and every night to begin your journey as a true princess.

Become a Princess with the
Official Princess Briana Royalty Pack

Choice of Princess Dress
Retail Price: $24.99

Tiara
Retail Price: $9.99

Princess Briana T-shirt
Retail Price: $19.99

Princess Briana Book
Paperback
Retail Price: $12.99

For a Special Low Price of $59.99 (While Supplies Last)
**Go to www.princessbriana.com to pre-order your Official Princess Briana Royalty Pack
today before they are sold out!!**

Printed in the United States
144015LV00002B